I0482881

From Homeless to Entrepreneur

How to Become Successful Entrepreneur

When You Are Homeless

Robert Rodgers, PhD

Olympia, Washington

Contents

Introduction

- **If you are in a desperate situation...**
- **If you currently have no home...**
- **If you have no money...**

you have likely resorted to begging. Admittedly, begging for donations from strangers does ultimately generate a little pocket change, if not a steady income for some people. My idea for transforming your life from being homeless and penniless today to sustaining a more comfortable, healthy and safe lifestyle tomorrow is to shift your orientation from being a beggar to becoming an entrepreneur.

Why? The reason is simple. You are bound to double if not triple the money you make from begging on the streets. Why is this so?

When you beg, there is no exchange of energy between the stranger who donates the money and you, the recipient of the gift. The person who donates money into your begging pot gives something to you – money – but you offer nothing in return.

One key reason people are willing to give money to beggars is that they get temporary infusion of pleasure. They have done a little something for someone who is in desperate need of assistance. The beggar gets the pocket change but does not offer anything in exchange other than an unhappy face and downtrodden look.

A one way energy exchange is not sustainable in the long run for any business. If the relationship does not involve a balance of giving and receiving it will quickly dissolve. In the begging business you cannot expect your customers to continue giving you money with no expectation of receiving anything in exchange.

The possibility of recruiting repeat customers is low. This business model is called begging for a reason. The beggar takes all and gives nothing in return. The exchange is unfair to your customers.

You can transform your business model from of begging to entrepreneur today. To do so, you must take one important step. You have to be willing to give something in exchange for the money people give to you. The principal of fair exchange is fundamental to all good business practices.

Businesses offer products and services that people are willing to pay money to get. The business gets the money. The customer pays a fair price for the product or service they receive. Each party gives something and gets something in return. The exchange is fair.

Better yet, when your customers like what you have to offer, they will come back time and time again. The idea that you will find threaded throughout this book is the principal of fair exchange. What do you have to offer right now to your customers?

The suggestions you will soon encounter in my little book are fueled by this terribly important principal of fair exchange. No money needs to be invested or spent to offer products or services right now. You simply have to decide to shift your business strategy from beggar to entrepreneur.

Once you transform your business approach from beggar to entrepreneur you will be pleasantly pleased with the outcome:

- You will earn more money.
- You will hold your head up with pride rather than shame.
- You will treasure the promise of better times ahead.
- You will allow hope to simmer in your heart for a better future for yourself and your family.

First allow me to sketch out the advantages and disadvantages of the begging business. I will then argue that shifting to an entrepreneurial business can be very advantageous and profitable in the long run.

Begging as a Business

What does begging as a business entail? No upfront funds or startup expenses required. Duh. Of course you say. I am homeless.

Duh yes I say, but what business exists that requires no upfront investment even if only a few hundred dollars? This is a huge incentive for anything. It is the primary reason who so many homeless people (and those who are not homeless) continue to beg on busy street corners day after day.

Even more impressive is the return on investment. With no initial investment required, your return is impressive indeed. No other business matches that return. Your business sees a 100% profit from all revenues received. Further, homeless people do not worry about paying taxes because the total income is so little.

Startup requirements involve constructing a make shift sign out of a scrap of cardboard. A plea for money is written on the sign which is held at chest level. The sign is designed to appeal to the sympathies of people who pass by.

Beggars set up their business at different locations. Some stand on street corners and consider their target market to be all people driving in automobiles. Others stand on downtown street locations and consider their target market to be downtown shoppers, business people and folks out for a good time.

While there is no question that the return on investment of the begging business is as good as it gets there are formidable challenges and obstacles.

- Sales are meager, often so small and insufficient that daily revenues do not cover living expenses.
- There is virtually no potential to expand the business and expect any predictable increase in revenues.
- The competition is stiff and aggressive. During tough economic times, a surprising number of people enter into the begging business. Because times are hard for everyone, fewer and fewer people are willing to make donations to the needy. In other words, the market shrinks as the number of providers sore.
- There is little competitive advantage to the begging business. For a business to succeed you have to offer an advantage

over your competitors, something that no one else offers. My observations of the begging business reveal that everyone follows the same business strategy which, admittedly, has proved modestly successful for some people. That is why so many people copy it.

Standard Practices in the Begging Business

- Dress as though you look homeless.

  It is important to wear old, dirty disheveled clothes so that you look the part of a person without money. This is not a difficult criteria to satisfy given that there are no funds available to purchase new clothes.

- Look pathetic as you hold your sign.

  This criteria is also not difficult to satisfy for most people who are homeless. It is near impossible to put on a cheery face when you have not slept for months or eaten good meal for days.

- Make a simple sign with large letters so people can read it easily

  The sign should not look professional. It needs to be credible. It should look like it was made by a person who has no money and is in fact homeless.

- Make a simple plea for money,

  People adopt different strategies: "Anything Helps" or "Disabled vet" or "My children are hungry. Please help"

- Say to people who pass by you "Got a quarter to spare?"

- Optional: Have a dog by your side as you beg.

  People are more like to give money to feed a starving dog than a human being who is hungry.

Why People Refuse to Give Money to Beggars

Some people have fine-tuned the business of begging. They are actually not homeless. They earn a reasonable income sufficient to support themselves to a modest lifestyle.

Some people believe this is the case for all beggars. This belief obviously cuts into the potential market share. They are convinced many of the people in the begging business are not homeless or penniless. It is simply their way of making a buck.

Other people believe that anyone can make a go of life if they simply set the intention. They believe people are homeless because they choose to be homeless. They think that the homeless have no interest in helping themselves. This belief is held by many people.

Still other people do not like the unfair exchange. They do not want to offer something of themselves (money) without receiving something in return.

The potential market share of people will to offer money to beggars is not that large! It also shrinks drastically as economic times get tough for everyone.

Begging Yields Poor Returns

OK. Begging is a business of sorts, but a business that offers meager returns. People who sell products on the internet can expect to a sales conversion for one to three out of a 100 visitors to their website. What are the odds in the begging business?

From my observations, beggars succeed in getting money from about 1 out of every 500 people who visit their location. This return is not even one out of one hundred. You chances of having a banner sales day are slim.

Worse, you run the risk of harassment by the police or by people who do not like it when they see people begging on the streets. Many cities are enacting strict laws that make begging a crime. Some city councils have decided that having beggars on the streets is bad for businesses. You can be put in jail for begging in some localities.

The truth about the begging business is that it offers few opportunities for expansion and little chance of earning enough money to sustain even a modest lifestyle. If you are new to the begging business you are competing with other experienced people who are adept at convincing people through their body language and signs to make a contribution. In short, the number of customers continues to dwindle as the number of highly seasoned competitors continues to expand. No business consultant would recommend you compete in such a market.

Why Not Become an Entrepreneur?

Why not shift from the shameful identity of a beggar to the prestigious identity of an entrepreneur? Becoming an entrepreneur is certainly a safer business and more lucrative than the business of begging. City councils do not put entrepreneurs in jail. They give them subsidies.

Entrepreneurs figure out how to help themselves. Doesn't it make good sense to adopt the identity of an entrepreneur rather being perceived as a helpless beggar who is targeted by the police for harassment and citizens with ridicule?

People do have violent reactions to beggars for one simple reason. There is a knowing deep inside that they could find themselves in the very same situation next year. They know that they may be rich today and broke tomorrow.

Why not approach the problem of homelessness you currently confront differently? Instead of hopping on the band wagon of the begging business because it appears in the moment there is no other alternative, consider a very different approach: Become an entrepreneur. Do it today.

Consider the reasons why it would be smart to abandon your current business practice of begging.

First, wouldn't you agree that it sounds a whole lot better to tell people you are an entrepreneur and not a beggar. Right? The energetic charge of the entrepreneurial identity is off the carts. The energetic charge of the identity of beggar is not even measurable.

Second, adopting the identity of entrepreneur gives you an instant infusion of hope for the future. Entrepreneurs are the movers and shakers of the world. They are the people who make lots of money and take vacations in exotic places. Anoint yourself as an entrepreneur and you too are on the road to becoming wealthy.

Most of the richest entrepreneurs have at one time or another been penniless too just like you. Many of the most successful entrepreneurs never even graduated from high school. At one time or another, most had just enough money to feed themselves for a day. That is no different from you right now. Right?

Most of the immigrants crossed the oceans and landed on the shores of the United States with little money and fewer resources. You know as well as I that many immigrants (who are our ancestors) became very wealthy.

Do a little check into your own family history and you will probably discover some of your ancestors emerged out of the depths of dire poverty to become very successful business people.

Successful entrepreneurs are no smarter than you! They just understood the importance of creating a fair exchange in their business. They gave to their customers a product or service. Their customers gladly gave them money in exchange.

Third, becoming an entrepreneur gives you instant credibility. Beggars have no credibility. They are viewed as the losers of society which, as you well know, is a bad rap. Entrepreneurs are the elite of society. They struck out on their own and made a go of it all.

If you insist on embracing the identity of beggar,   your health is bound to deteriorate. And your ability to feed yourself and your family will be severely compromised. Embracing the business strategy of beggar pretty much guarantees that you will continue to be homeless. It reinforces the feelings of hopelessness and helplessness. If there is no hope, there is little chance you can turn your current situation around.

Your energy will be drained throughout each day because you are taking from other people and not giving anything in return. Why would your existing customers continue to give you money so you can drain more of their energy? When you take from others and do not give back you are draining people's life force. They will not continue giving you money week after week unless they get off on being miserable themselves. Yes, there is a market there but it is thin.

The pathway to sustaining your energy, building wealth and reclaiming your health is to fuel the endless fire of energy within yourself.

That happens with entrepreneurs. They light a fire inside their soul. Do the same. Watch your life transform helplessness and hopelessness into a life of security, joy and endless pleasure.

Don't Entrepreneurs Need Money and Resources to Start Their Business?

No. The belief entrepreneurs need funds to launch a business is a myth. Most entrepreneurs started with nothing - just like the position you find yourself in right now. They did not begin with fancy bank loans. Banks do not lend money to people who are just starting out. They lend money to businesses that are already successful.

What is Stopping You from Becoming an Entrepreneur Today?

You do not need to earn a degree to declare yourself an entrepreneur. Entrepreneurs do not have degrees. Most are not even high school graduates. The only criteria that needs to be met is for you to decide right here and now that you want to transform you existing habits of begging to offering a business that offers your customers value for the money they give to you.

As one party to the exchange you receive a contribution usually in the form of money (or some other donation like food). What does your customer get in return for their contribution? When the exchange is fair they receive something that is of value to them. In other words, there is a fair exchange between the parties.

Fair Exchange

If you are homeless at the present time and purse a begging business my question is this:

What do you give in exchange for the money you get when you beg?

- Are you entertaining people with your sad looks of despair?

- Are you helping people solve their problems?
- Are you offering helpful information?
- Are you making people laugh out loud (and thus help them manufacture dopamine which makes them high and happy?
- Are you selling them products that will solve their problems?

Of course the answer to all of these questions is no if you are a beggar. If you are homeless, you are not giving anything in exchange for the money or donations people give you. You are taking from others but not giving anything in return.

I suspect you are probably thinking right now …

> *"I have nothing to give in exchange for the money people give me."*

Really? Do you really believe that? That belief is dead wrong. Of course you have something to offer. I will outline in the next section a number of ways you can offer something to people and receive a fair exchange in the form of money.

Summary

The way to transform rags to riches is to shift your thinking. Stamp out the mistaken belief that the only choice for you is to take from others since you have nothing to give. Receive into your heart, mind and soul the true belief that you have an endless bounty of gifts to share that people will gladly pay money to see, experience or receive. Once you succeed in transforming the truth of who you are, you will be well on your way to becoming a successful entrepreneur.

Best of all – you can become an entrepreneur today. You can begin your business right now. No upfront funding is required. No investment is needed. No long term planning is necessary. You do not need a strategic business plan. You simply have to decide to take action today.

The principal here is simple. You have to figure out something you can offer to others in exchange for the money people give to you. Stop expecting that people should give something to you without a fair exchange.

Best of all, when people like what you have to offer, they will come back for more. They will become your repeat customers because they are eager to pay you for the service or product you have to offer. Think of each passerby as a potential long term customer, not a sucker you will never see again. You are no longer conning people to give you something. You are offering something to people that they want or need.

How to Become a Successful Entrepreneur

What follows is a collection of business ideas that you could initiate today with no money down. These ideas can potentially generate a much better income for you than begging.

See if just one of these suggestions calls out to you. Each of my ideas for a new business are all just initial possibilities that may well lead to bigger and even more profitable businesses. They all involve a fair exchange between you and your customers. Consider now some of the many possibilities:

A Dime for the Punchline

As noted earlier the standard practice among the homeless is to create a makeshift sign that looks like it has been written and created by someone who does not have a cent to their name. The signs are hand written in large letters with words often misspelled. The idea is to elicit an emotion of empathy. The word among the homeless is that the more pathetic looking the sign, the better the return.

How about a different approach? Create a different sign that has a more professional look to it. If you cannot write legibly, recruit a friend who can.

At the top of your sign - write in large letters

A Nickel for the Punchline

Then - write the first part of a joke. A new joke can be prepared each day – but example might be:

Knock, Knock!

Who's there?

Albie.

Albie who?

When you get the 5 cent donation - you say:

"Albie out here if you need me."

In other words - you get the donation and the customer gets to laugh at the punch line, Get it? Your customer gets to be entertained. There is a fair exchange here. Your client is a customer, not a sucker. If they like the joke they get to tell the joke to one of their friends. That is well worth a nickel to anyone.

Better yet - if your jokes are really funny - you will get repeat customers.

Here is the best part. Your customers will often not just give you a nickel for the punchline. The surprise is that they will often throw into the change can much more change than a nickel. They want to reward you for your creative effort.

Now, I have used a simple knock knock joke as an example. There are thousands and thousands of simple jokes that you can use. Of course you will have to put up a new joke up every day because many of the same people pass by.

How can you generate a reasonable income every day with this approach? Personalize your jokes. After all, comedians make a great living making fun of them. You can too. You may find yourself on a late night TV show as the homeless person who got famous.

Now, when I say personalize the jokes, what do I mean exactly?

- Are you a blond woman? Why not create a new blond joke every day and make fun of yourself? People will love it.
- Are you bald? There are lots of funny bald jokes which are all the funnier when you make fun of yourself.
- Are you homeless? Duh. Need I say more?
- Are you handicapped or Chinese or wear thick glasses or ...

There are thousands of brief, snappy jokes for just about every situation and person. If you are poking fun of yourself, you stand to make a steady income. You might even be featured in the local newspaper or in local blogs. Don't be surprised if you discover that some people will drive out of their way just to hear your joke of the day for a nickel.

Yes. You do have to make up a new sign every day. Yes. You do have to think up a new joke every day. Where can you find good jokes? Do searches on the free computers at the downtown public library.

Jokes are a nickel a dozen. Right? Get paid for your good work. Get rewarded for your creativity. This will be a lot more fun for you than standing on your street corner station looking pathetic so people will take pity on you.

Become a Statute that Moves Only When Paid

In some US cities like San Francisco some people make a surprisingly good income by dressing up in some interesting costume and then posing as a still statute that does not move unless they are paid to do so. People love to look at people standing still to see if they can make them twitch or laugh or giggle or move.

Here is how this can work for you. Perhaps it is a hot summer day. On this particular day you can wear a short sleeve shirt. Designate a small performance stage on your favorite downtown sidewalk that does not block or obstruct foot traffic.

Put a tin can on the ground (which can be a recycled can from the garbage). Beside the can place a sign with large letters that reads:

I Move for a Quarter

Then - stand perfectly still in a posed position. Do not move or twitch or smile. Stand just like the colorful guards at Buckingham Palace in London. No movement. No smiles. No grins. No contact with the public.

When you hear a jingle in the tin cup - shift to a new position. As you move, be sure to look at the person who gave the money straight in the eyes. Offer a warm smile of gratitude for their donation.

© Zero Point Healers

Of course, some people may only throw a quarter into your can. Most will toss more money. And guess what? When you offer your customer a warm, connected smile as you move, many people will often throw extra change in the pot even after they have already given the 25 cents just to see you move.

When you start this new business you will have to wear whatever clothes you have available. You do not have to acquire a new outfit to start. Like any successful entrepreneur you can choose to upgrade into a costume when you have the resources. If you wear an interesting costume you will make a lot more money.

Many of the people who do this work in San Francisco are not even homeless. This is their business. It can be your business too if you like to have a little fun and don't mind standing still for long periods.

So, after you generate a little extra income you will have a few dollars to invest in a costume. Depending on who you are, dress up like a character everyone knows: Snow White,

Cinderella, Elvis, Michael Jackson - anyone who might be a character others would recognize.

You may not have to even invest a few dollars in a costume. Chances are pretty good that you can find props or clothes that have been thrown away by others. Goodwill sells great clothes and costumes at cheap prices. Be sure to go on the discount days.

Once you see that this form of entertainment works for you, why not create a little more sophisticated costume? If your costume is interesting people will come from miles just to see you. You may become the most interesting happening downtown and attract large crowds. Best of all, people will gladly toss a little money in your can for the entertainment.

Smiles Make Me Happy

Did you know that people will give money for smiles? They do. OK. I get the fact that you are in no position to be happy. I really do understand that the last thing you want to do is to smile to other people.

I can also assure you that actors do not feel like showing the feelings they have display in certain scenes when they are filmed - but that is the job. They get paid good money for showing certain feelings (like smiling!) even when they do not feel like it.

You can too even if in the moment you feel depressed and downtrodden. You can make a sign
that says:

Smiles Make Me Happy!

And then, you offer a very large and impressive smile to each and every person who passes by you.

I suggest that you simply wait for people to offer you money. You would be surprised how a simple smile can offer an important uplift to people who may be having a particularly difficult day. Here you are homeless and you can smile at them! WOW!

People may pass you by for weeks and not give any money. But, if they see you smiling each time they pass by, don't be surprised if one day they stop and give a generous donation for the wonderful service you have rendered.

Yes, it takes some energy from you to smile all day long. The best news of all is that smiling will help you also feel better. You are giving yourself a continual healing throughout the day and earning money as well. No investment required.

Sell Pet Rocks

Fifty years ago an entrepreneur decided to sell rocks. The rocks did not cost him anything. They collected the rocks for free from the earth. This entrepreneur boxed up the rocks, called them *Pet Rocks*, put a price of $2.50 on each one and made a fortune.

Rocks are magical crystals that emerge from mother earth. They carry with them energy that can be beneficial to people. Why not sell rocks?

If it worked for one entrepreneur it can work for you too!

It will certainly help to collect a variety of rocks of different shapes and sizes. It will also help to examine each rock and decide what energy that rock might convey to your customers. Put labels on the rocks like

Hold me each day and I will help you ...

- Find love
- Make money
- Pay off debt
- Find happiness
- Heal my wounds
- Heal cancer

You get the point. Rocks emit different energies. With a little practice, you may even be good at guessing which rocks convey which type of energy. And of course, place a price tag on each rock.

Some rocks should cost more than others! Do this for a month or two and you will soon be widely known throughout the city as the Rock

© Zero Point Healers

Lady (or Rock Man). Now that is a much more distinctive title than the homeless guy, eh?

You may be thinking – you have to be kidding me. People will not pay for rocks. I know of people who have paid for rocks. Give it a try. You may be surprised at the outcome. Don't just lay the rocks out on the ground. Market them!

Play a Musical Instrument

Are you a musician? Everyone is familiar with the musicians on street corners who perform with a hat at their feet. Consider refining this business by adding a few extras that people will pay for.

List popular songs on a sign that says - I will gladly play any of these songs for you. Just ask people who pass by what song they would like to hear. Be sure to include romantic songs.

Most musicians just play the music they know and like. What does your audience want to hear? Who is passing by your station? One potentially lucrative approach is to check into each person and speculate what song might appeal to them. Connect with them. Play that song. The connection will make the difference between getting a contribution or watching the person walk on by.

Again, you are offering a fair exchange. People get to hear your beautiful music. In exchange they drop a dollar or two in the hat. They feel good about their donation. You feel good about having a chance to play music and get paid for it. That is what a fair exchange is all about.

Juggling

OK. So you have never juggled balls or oranges or apples before? You have no idea how to juggle? Why not practice while you are standing on the street corner?

There are books at your public library that give juggling instructions that can offer you great tips on how to get started.

You may be shocked at how good at you can get at juggling with a little practice. The better you can juggle, the more money you will make. You will soon be widely known as the Juggler on Main Street.

Mr. Pardo

Create a makeshift puppet which can be easily made from sock. This happens to be the same material that was used to make some of the famous Muppet puppets.

Make a professional sign that says:

"Mr. Pardo [or whatever name you want to call your puppet] will insult you if you ask him."

Now become a puppeteer. You are the one saying the insult - but Mr. Pardo (your puppet) is the one who offers the insult.

Your customer will look at the puppet, not at you. In other words, become a ventriloquist.

Believe it or not, some people love to be insulted. Really. If your customer loves the insult they will drop some change into the donation bucket you can position at your feet. You will probably make more money the more outrageous the insult.

There is no need to ask for a donation. If people enjoy the insults they will gladly volunteer a donation. You will soon be widely known as Mr. Pardo. If people do not like to be insulted they will not ask.

Clean Team

One entrepreneurial business you can launch today is cleaning up your download city or town. Why bother to get serious about cleaning up the sidewalks and streets when you are not getting paid anything? There are several reasons:

Cleaning is a legitimate business that pays well. It will offer you and all the other homeless in your town an opportunity to transform attitudes toward the homeless.

If you are cleaning up the downtown streets you are no longer free loaders looking for a handout. You are giving something of yourself to help your town. You are helping keep it squeaky clean.

As an aside, several internet businesses have recently sold for several billion dollars that have never generated a cent of revenue. My point is simple. Doing something for free in the beginning can result in huge returns down the line.

Get together with several other people who are currently homeless. Name the new business whatever you like. A name I like is the "Clean Team" or "Sidewalk Smart" or "[name of town} Clean." In my city your business would be known as "Olympia Clean".

Next, tie a green cloth around your arm so people can identify you as a member of the

"Clean Team". Some people who pass by will begin to ask - what is everyone I see wearing that green cloth on their arm?

The word will eventually get out as to who you are and what you are doing. You are not one of the homeless. You are a member of a new downtown business known as the Clean Team. You are a citizen volunteer who cares about your city.

Depending on how many people are willing to participate, divide up the town into blocks, assign each person a section of the city to clean. It could be only one or two blocks.

Make a simple sign that says –

Proud Member of Clean Team

Be sure to place a receptacle (or can) next to the sign for people to make donations.

Each team member needs to monitor their block closely by picking up trash, cigarettes and other mess that finds its way onto the streets.

Who is going to pay for this work? You might be surprised. Business owners will love the fact that you are keeping the sidewalks clean. They are potential long term customers. They no longer have to sweep outside their stores. They may eventually pay you a weekly sum to keep their store fronts clean. Who knows? The job might evolve into one of cleaning windows or even their stores. Clean this week and become a full time employee tomorrow!

This will transform people's attitudes toward your presence on the streets. Yes, you are homeless. Yes, you have no money right now. But yes, you are making a positive difference to the overall appearance of the town. Everyone will become more tolerant of your presence. This will make it much easier if you have to sleep on the streets at night, won't it?

This is just the beginning. I suggest that after you get organized and have several months of experience working as a team. Then, make a presentation before the city/town council.

In your presentation assemble all members of your team. Elect a spokesperson who explains that you have started a new business which is dedicated to keeping the city squeaky clean.

Your initial presentation informs the council of your new business.

The presentation may well give you a lot of good press. Good press means that when people see you cleaning up the streets they will be more likely to pay for your generous volunteer services through their donations. You are giving people a valued service. They are giving you money. You are giving them a city they can be proud of. Once again, there is a fair exchange here.

I suggest that you plan on making regular, brief presentations before your city/town council with updates on your progress. Start making small request after a few months. For example, ask for the use of a few brooms perhaps. After everyone is impressed with your initiative, ask for the use of a pressure washer to wash the sidewalks.

Where will all this lead? It can only result in a positive outcome for members of the Clean Team as well as the city/town. If your team keeps the streets squeaky clean, you might even be surprised that the city council or downtown business association might be willing to pay your team money for your efforts (though this outcome would likely take time to happen). Time would be required to build trust.

Even if this is not the outcome, you have created a bounty of good will that will ease the challenge considerably of having to be homeless at the present time.

Magic Tricks

Learn a few magic tricks. You can perform the tricks as people pass by on the street. The best tricks are those that appeal to children. If you entertain children in a safe and nonthreatening way their parents will often pay you to entertain their children (and them)!

The public library is filled with the secrets behind all great magic tricks. You only need a few tricks every week to succeed. People will get to know you as the magician and will go out of their way to see what you have in store for them. Children will beg their parents to visit the magician to see what he/she has up their sleeve today!

Sell Tee-shirts

There are a surprising number of business opportunities you can take advantage using the internet. They require no money down. By way of example, one approach is explained on the website titled www.teespring.com

Teespring is a unique way for you to design and sell custom apparel online like tea shirts on their internet website. You design a product and sell it. The shirts you design will be connected to a time sensitive event. For example, marathons or art fairs or music festivals are great events for tee shirts.

No upfront funds are required to get started in this business. Sales of your tee shirts pay for the production and shipping of your product. When you use Teespring you don't have to pay a dollar upfront, guess how many shirts you'll need, or have to chase anyone down for cash.

It only takes a couple of minutes to launch a campaign and start selling awesome merchandise on Teespring. The company makes the t shirts and ships them to buyers. You collect the profits.

This is only one example of how you can make money on the internet. There are also lots of people out there who offer free training programs that tell you how to make money on the internet with no money down. Most public libraries have computers you can use at least for one hour a day, often longer. Use them to make money.

If you are a writer, you can publish your own book with no money down. Daniel Hall offers regular free training over the internet on how to self-publish your books.

http:/realfastbook.com

Are You So Depressed, Sick and Hungry that You Cannot Even Think Straight?

I fully understand and honor the reality that your circumstances at the present time are horrible. I understand that your energy is depleted and your health is compromised.

Mounting the energy and strength to shift your current focus from the helpless victim to successful entrepreneur is a huge challenge. I understand that it is nearly impossible to get motivated to provide a service when you have not eaten for several days.

I also realize that many of you are victims of circumstances that were far beyond your control. You probably never expected you would be in the circumstances you currently confront.

Here is the truth of your situation. If you cannot mount the energy to shift your focus from victim (as a person with a begging business) to entrepreneur, the likelihood you will work your way out of your current circumstances is slim indeed.

You are the only person who can save yourself right now. Why not just gut it out? Why not give the entrepreneurial approach a trial run? There is a strong economic incentive to make the shift today.

People who are entrepreneurs have resources. They make good money. Some are very wealthy. Why not merge into the high profile energy of success rather than latching onto the dark and potentially harmful energy of being a beggar?

Begging is not and will never be a successful business. Join the ranks of people who are successful. Many have found themselves in your very same circumstances.

Did you find any of my suggestions for new businesses appealing? If not, design your own business that takes advantage of your strengths and abilities. What are your skills? Build on those as your create a new service or product to offer.

It is true that you will have to put out some extra effort, thought and planning to offer a product or service to your potential market. Aren't you putting out a great deal of energy right now with little return for your time, effort and focus?

Once you shift your business plan from beggar to entrepreneur dozens of good ideas will begin to float into your consciousness. I have offered only a sampling of ideas to light up your thinking cap..

What are your skills?

What do you like to do?

Create a simple service or product right now. Try it out tomorrow. To be quite clear, the first attempts may not be terribly successful. That is precisely what happens to all businesses. Keep inventing new strategies if the current idea does not succeed. Try out new business ventures. Give each idea time to succeed.

Some people who pay for your service – even if it is only to smile at you as you drive past your street corner every day – may only pay for your service after they see you smiling every day for a month. Why not let a simple smile help make someone's day tomorrow? People will gladly pay your for the service or product that offers them value.

Build a customer base of people who will continue to come back for more rather than expect that each new person you encounter is a one shot opportunity. Built a new business where people will intentionally drive past your street corner (or wall down your sidewalk) to grab that delicious smile, service or product you have to offer.

Perhaps the biggest incentive to shift your business approach from beggar to entrepreneur is to reduce harassment by police. What police officer would harass a citizen who is offering their services for free to clean up downtown? You are a citizen volunteer, not a helpless homeless person.

What city council would be inclined to enact laws that offer no support to the homeless if the homeless people create an interesting and vibrant downtown that attracts visitors and generates additional sales for businesses? You and your colleagues have the time and the talent to create an environment of entertainment and experience that can make any town or city unique.

Are You Waiting to Land a Full Time Job?

Are you waiting around to secure a paid job from a company? There is a slim chance you will succeed these days. Let me not discourage this possibility. But the future of employment across the globe rests with individuals who create their own businesses as they develop new and innovative products and services to offer.

The hay day of the large corporation is about to come to an end. Most people – homeless or not – will have to resort to becoming an entrepreneur. The truth is that anyone over 50 these days has a slim chance of being employed by any company, homeless or not.

The Best Time to Start a New Business is Right Now

Why not start your business right now? Whatever direction you decide to pursue, remember the principal that must be satisfied to be successful. Create a new business for yourself that offers a fair exchange between you and your customers. When a fair exchange exists, the opportunities for growth and expansion are limitless. I look forward to seeing you featured on a late night talk show soon.

www.ingramcontent.com/pod-product-compliance
Lightning Source LLC
Chambersburg PA
CBHW071825170526
45167CB00003B/1426